LIGN SERIES / 2

The Great Book of the Woods

Gerry Loose

XYLEM BOOKS 2020

Gerry Loose, *The Great Book of the Woods*
First published in 2020 by Xylem Books

All content © Gerry Loose 1977–2020
The author's moral rights have been asserted
This edition © Xylem Books 2020

ISBN: 978-1-9999718-9-2

Xylem Books is an imprint of Corbel Stone Press

INTRODUCTION

Ogham is a rune-like script of the early Irish language found on standing stones made between the 4th and 8th centuries CE. It comprises strokes across or to either side of a central stem line. Each stroke now represents a letter of the Gaelic *Beith-luis-nin* 'alphabet'. It is found on monoliths mainly in Ireland, with some in Scotland, and some dual-text ogham/Latin stones in Wales. There are also inscriptions other than the monolithic – on tools or in caves – but these are rare.

There are numerous myths concerning the script's origins: that it was invented to keep secrets from the Roman conquerors of nearby Britain; that it was similarly invented to keep secrets from the lands that Ireland was later to annexe as Dal Riada (the islands and mainland of western Scotland); that it was invented by an obscure 4th century CE Christian sect. It is also said in some quarters that it was handed down by, or named for, Ogmos, the Celtic god of eloquence.

There are many methods of interpreting ogham. The script itself is steeped in the secrecy of the literate over the non-literate. It is therefore always regarded as the property of the high poets, the early medieval *fili* of Ireland, who would spend many years memorising up to fifty ways of reading or deciphering it. The poetic possibilities are therefore manifold.

The *Auraicept na n-Éces – The Scholars' Primer –*
perhaps dates to the 7th century CE and is a discussion of
various grammatical matters, together with ogham tracts
from other, later, sources. *The Primer* itself is the earliest
vernacular treatment of grammar, meanings of words,
origin of languages and poetic judgement. It is also a
juxtaposition of grammar and the natural world, with
constant reference to trees and wood. Indeed, the most
widely known and quoted ogham tract is the ogham tree
alphabet, which attributes a particular tree or plant to
each letter of the Gaelic *Beith-luis-nin.*

The author of *The Primer* discusses a comparison of
grammar with the Tower of Babel, a discussion which
maintains that Gaelic, being the last invented language,
after Hebrew, Greek and Latin, among the seventy two
languages found at the Tower, incorporates every sound
in every language and is therefore the most comprehen-
sive and finest language in which thought and poetry
may be expressed. Later additions to *The Primer* are the
texts of ogham tracts taken from the *Book of Ballymote,*
the *Yellow Book of Lecan* and the text of the 'Trefhocul'
from the *Book of Leinster –* books which were all medieval collections of genealogy, history, poetry, biography,
grammar, prayers, lists, medicine and Christianity, as
well as ogham, all written in Middle Irish.

My approach has been to base my ogham poems on
readings of the phrase-oghams of both Morainn Mac

Main and Mac Ind Oic, as given in the medieval texts
in the books mentioned above. I've also given sideways
glances to the *tree, divination* and *naming* oghams. It is
clear from my own readings that a narrative of a pastoral
society is being recorded (or perhaps codified messages
in pastoral phrases). The culture becomes apparent as
highly sophisticated, close to the earth; a transhumance
society with a keen awareness of landscape, habitat, trees
and plants – part and parcel of the Sweeney stories, the
Tain bo Culaigne, the *Annals of Ulster*. A first and last
recorded flowering of a civilisation dating from Bronze
Age Ireland, and perhaps much earlier.

As letters on the inscribed stones are sometimes dou-
bled up, I have used this for emphasis. Similarly, as not
all words in Gaelic have precise English equivalents (for
example *seanachas* – the body of cultural knowledge –
has overtones of biography, tradition, genealogy, history
and language), I have moved between phrase oghams to
use words that I think work best in a given poem. Where
these will not do, I have used other, appropriate trans-
lations of the Gaelic, and the stone and the landscape
itself, to make a viable poem in English from the ogham.

The poems here are therefore versions, creative
re-inventions and co-creations, made with other poets
and translators who lived from the 4th to the 14th
centuries CE.

NOTES ON THE TEXT

Ogham is usually read from left to right if horizontal, bottom to top if vertical.

Letters at the bottom of each ogham page are the Roman alphabet equivalents of each inscription, spelling out the ogham strokes.

The Great Book of the Woods

Versions from the ogham
& from the Auraicept na n-Éces

THE PRIMER

let profit be *gno*
let *bora* be strength
let the duality of the conjugal be *ter*
let *rfoph* be veneration
let piety be *brops*
rihph be cheerfulness
let *gal* be a kingdom
let religion be *fkal*
let *clitps* be nobility
let dignity be *mymos*
let *fann* be recognition
let honour be *ulio*
let *gabpal* be compliance
blaqth be sunlight
rain be *merc*
let *pal* be day & night
let peace be *gatrb*
biun be water & fire
let longevity be *spax*

o

the present time is put for all times
a deed wonderful unlawful
he confounded them
he confused them
when one would say to another
fetch me a stone
it was a stick he'd bring

o

on that account
the select language
the additional language
the language parted related
in the Great Book of the Woods

○

what is the language parted
in the Great Book of the Woods?
this: óig & máir
this: náir & náir mas
other is amuis & gairg
& grin
what is the verb?
it is this: shining
coming & showing
there is science in place
it comes out of the letters
into words

o

fall, shine, show, come
out of that primary nature into words
out of these letters into words
they speak the thing
the foundation of the voice
the ways of the voices
the letter is a road
a voice path
they make the voice in place

o

the wood vowels
that nourish while in mind
that sing at giving
that sue for reward
that judge greatness or smallness
that sit after payment
the material for words
is cut out of them
the sides of oaks

o

half the voice is thrown out
the stammering voice
the half voice place
the half voice way
not because they would be
speechless altogether
the mutes
before them & after them
before them & after them

o

he the man
she the woman
it the heaven
speech-way
along the way
along the path
which is trodden
let it come
let it go
he is the heavens
she is the stone
it is the head
her nose or her eye
his tooth or his mouth
words of a language
we do not know
we do not think sweet
we do not use them
she is the steed
a bark of butter
a sieve of corn

o

what is comparison of sense without sound?
what is comparison of sound without sense?
comparison of sense & sound together
that is the proper comparison
there is good & nothing to surpass
its measure to suit the ear
its adjustment to breathing
a wood of science
a mark of aspiration
letter to letter

o

the space of time
between
two syllables
is its meaning
is a letter a species?
in the wood of the forest
is a letter a genus?

o

according to sound
which goes
which comes
the fragment
of cut off air
diminution of time
the tongue of silence
double sounds
knowledge of thing perishes
unless the name is known
power & want of power
full power & half power
written & not counted
stone turning music
they step

o

poison of a serpent
they blow the fire
meal of corn
heaven round earth
the staves of words
interloping syllables
plain of deer
copses of wood
duck along a pool
swift & dense flax seed

o

ear-lobe compression
family-like-every-second-one-of them
all-the-mistakes-which-we-have-committed

     ○

a thing is not an origin for itself
syllables
choral song silent in its law
the music that is
small music that is humming
loud music trumpeting
its mournful cry
thunder or a tree
when it is a whistle
shriller harder
greater music when a harp
silent its music
when sweetest it is silent

o

the limbs of science are named
not mixed speech
it praises from the front
it is sent
it is hastened
staves of words
a staff out of a word
staves in reasonable speech
in the mouths
halting from word to word

o

the interloping syllable
its flinging of a man
if a man suffer on land
the man allows suffering on him
he goes afterwards
to bathe himself in the water
he lets himself down the bank
into the water
tot says the wave under him
the sound which waves make
the heavy voice the man utters
dropping himself on the water

o

the name has happened
to the sound
the haft of speech
from which no speech grows
but speech of death
the spear point
what is haft
which is after blade
the after blade
which is haft
& the haft
which is before blade
haft is the spear
haft itself will come
after blade
everything final
haft which is after blade
the haft is the haft
which is before blade

o

it is the head
it is artificial to say it
while it is on the man
it is natural to say it
after striking the head off him

o

the couple of the gore
redness & crimson
leg & foot
the couple of supporting
eyelashes & eyebrow
root & breadth
skin & sinew
activity & surface
one for warding upon
one for good warding
cap on knee
lips in strength & loudness
flesh & blood
which is in the flesh
top bone & jaw bones
knuckles & hair
a woman's limbs
are made of science

o

on, under, through, in
past the heavens
its interloping syllable
heaven about earth
cloud & bow of heaven
for every sort of speech
that is produced
on human lips

o

FIVE TREES

BIRCH

├

every sound that exists in every speech

APPLE

Ⅲ

Q

bush of leaf shreds
gestures of blood
fuse of the wretched
hinds' aurora
moon-afflicted protector

WILLOW

bloom & catkin
sallow & sallow
bees' thunder
honey river
water song

WHITETHORN

⊣

hound assembly
wolf assembly
terrible black
night raven
salmon spine

ASH

‡

O

horse wounder
horse lover
world dreamer
mouth of lightning
vowel in the mouth

INCHMARNOCK SONGS

HAVING REACHED THE HOLY REWARD

B L F S N H D T C Q

Her body fades with her hair becomes invisible her skin
       is a salmon.
Singing eye sings her songs together kine alpine kine
       grazing.
Guarded life is guarded shielded ringed with soldiers.
South from our slit ribs bees swarm north.
Now is elsewhere jealousy did this.

Thieves clean her breasts.
A bower is constructed high in the thorn.
Three fires jealousy love & death maggot us.
Under no place there are no trees there is no place.
Pulse great throbbing blooded heart harts live in her
       irises.

GAMING BOARD
(to be read in any direction)

B O H B A D A

A L A H B H

you're blest
you're fading

you're hopeful
shit shit

you're hopeful
shit shit

o sweet
you're flying

you're dead
concentrate

you're hopeful
shit shit

o pale
you're fleeing

you're blest
you're fading

you're hopeful
shit shit

you're chiselling
will it hold

you're dead
concentrate

you're dead
concentrate

counting chickens
shit shit

you're hopeful
shit shit

o pale
you're fleeing

a corpse
you're fading

o sweet
you're flying

you're hopeful
shit shit

you're hopeful
shit shit

you're hopeful
shit shit

you're dead
concentrate

o pale
you're fleeing

THE QUESTIONING

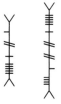

IAGH

CBGGAI

when does timber wither in oakwoods
at a flaying

what is sweeter than ivy grasses
flesh

what is torn apart drained
ash

what dances from a corpse mouth
salmon

what is torn apart drained
vein

what is ash salmon
grasses

what is grass ivy
a flaying

when does timber wither in oakwoods

BLACKWATERFOOT, ARRAN, KING'S CAVE

MAQI

son: to leave

friend: to stroll among trees

work: to ride stallions

killing: to be swift

father: to shelter the hunted

BLACKWATERFOOT, ARRAN, KING'S CAVE

VUEDLA

skinsilver birch
rowan of pillage
heather the udder brusher
poplar the horse trembler
oak of hill & adze
answer
song

SCOONIE

EDDARRNONN

no name for   them
they grow   deep within
tree proud   bush proud
urgent   they 're allies
though   they   groan
shrivel   in the hunt
still bigger than a horse

INCHYRA

INEHHETESCIETINNE

begin with honey
& fellowship of trees
one third of a spear
& a shroud

return salmon
return sun
return spring well
bees are dying

MAINS OF AFFORSK

NECTONIRE

beauty's a boast
& kinship with saplings

with red temper
& warriors' gear

cherished hazel
& grace disappear

cypher unknown
& wisdom undone

POLTALLOCH

CRONAN

there is a murmuring
such beauty
the rose redness that grows in a woman's face
the intensest of blushes

      equally wounding
      sense comes to her when she goes to her death

the noise is made
the noise made in delirium
the noise made marvelling
the noise is made

when she goes to her death sense
death enfolds her
a sheltering hind

DUNADD

FINN

the people of the boar will pass this way
& leave their print

above

        his vital force
        our ally

        our ally
        a destroying force

below

        from the earth

        his vital force
        the head   the emblem
        the back fit to break
        our ally

to the red face
the reddened face
to the fear white face
a force of freedom

KEISS BAY

NEHTETRI

daughters of the four winds
no more sleep

liberation
makes friends
like a hound her pups
like coals to a fire
friends
like emptiness filled
three times
it fires the blood
it lasts forever

on the stone from the
MOOR OF CARDEN
AT LOGIE ELPHINSTONE

QVTQU

twice sloe shield crescent moon & alder

thirty cattle welcome the shade

      (they're hot)

sixty cattle welcome the shade

      (they're thirsty)

cows strippers heifers yearlings stirks welcome the shade

      they welcome the shade of the fairest tree

dappled light on the brindled cows

delights the eye

this is for the growing of plants of stalks of stems of boles of
   trees

my eye is delighted

by dappled brindled cows

       in oak tree shade

cows heifers stirks calves in shade

thirty head

sixty head

fine beasts

fine tree

the yew wound with ivy
GIGHA

the old man speaks

nothing.	*fires gone*
shrivelled old wood	
no life.	*no zip of bees at the hive mouth*
cold houses	*the moss grows*
my shame	*my pain*
dying	*an effort*
my pain	*the light*
no bustle	*no spark*
no life.	*no bees*
cold houses	*moss*
nothing sweeter than grasses	*ivy*
shrivelled old wood	
no rest	
shrunken old wood	*no sap*

BRANDSBUTT

IRATADDOARENS

the ninth one the bleeding yew of Brynach period storms

the oldest wood
in the oldest wood

                    brings blood from sap
                    brings mouth corner

mutterings
the brought blood hot as coals

                    begins answering
                    side mouthing the logging

fraught as menstrual blood

                    begins blitz & serpent
                    mouthing of sap & blood

& the allies of wood
cut off a breast & fight

& death
busy as a bee

TY'N Y WLAD, CRICKHOWELL

TURPILI MOSAC TRALLONI

curses developers & keens wild land

unsung
            rivers   hills   woods

in stone houses
red faced at the fire   burning
the sweetest of wood from
the veteran woods   eye's delight

it's not the beginning of an answer
            even the strongest of effort
                        burning after slashing
                                    ploughs behind horses
it's not the beginning of an answer
            busy   busy
it doesn't begin to answer

there was stillness
bath   food   fire

damn the herders & red faced farmers

how smoothly the woods are gone
            sweet hag woods
                        apples of my eye
                                    my darlings

KNOCKSHANAWEE SOUTERRAIN

COLLI

how they all root-hum through hazel
fair sweet friends of nutshells
the ash which yellowing is also
become gorse smooth horse-stabber
guerrilla gear & skill
spewing flame-herbs & herb-flame
kye-food kye-friend-flame
parasite-eyebright or
drip of honey from corpse-gob
sallow & quicken & yew & you

BALLYKNOCK

ANM MEDDOGENI

from the branch
& from the fork of the branch
my name
born of mead

from exhalation
& from the deception of love
my name
born of wine

among the discerning
& in among their discourse
my name
unknown

PALIMPSESTS & RIDDLES

KNOCKSHANAWEE SOUTERRAIN

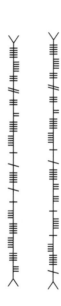

VEQIKAMIMAQILUGUNI

MICANAVVIMAQILUGUNI

a trick of the neck
is yew to pine

a trick of lungs
is pine to alder

a ruse of the voice track
is alder to yew

a trick of love
is brother to brother

a trick of darklight divine
is twin to twin

KNOCKSHANAWEE SOUTERRAIN RIDDLE

U C A N A V I M A L N

it is cold
is there frost

there are thorns
are they pricking

there is a resolution
is it legion

there is clamour
is there silence

the wood is ancient
is it withered

there are crypts
is it an effort

BALLYKNOCK SHORT DISCOURSE

right to the marrow
flame & steel

elegant & forthright
oldest & coldest

felloe & tang
vanguard & bevy

pine & groan
swaddle & mass grave

BALLYKNOCK RIDDLE

COVALUTI

sing us thorn
cleave us friend

not complaint
not rebuttal

soothe us horse
smooth us work

not effort
in soil

shelter us hind
sing us strength

flesh & grass
twining

BALLYKNOCK LETTERS SWIMMING

ERCAIDANA

hazel & pine then oak
start with these

their twists & torques
sisters to birch

they are the red boast
of sibling women

calling & scolding
sparks from speckled fire

BALLYKNOCK FROM THE LUNGS

ACTOMAQIMAGO

the ash field
the oldest energy

the path of the voice
iron rod of breath

the driving of slaves
a proverb of slaughter

one third wheel
one third weapon

begin your answer, pine
call your nut-marrow, hazel

BALLYKNOCK RIDDLE

ACTOMAQIMAGO

what thorn
& who's a friend of lesion

what work is smooth
& who helps geldings

what guards
& who spills

what is simplicity
& who delights in kine

what lives cold
& who cultivates plants

what pain
& who replies

CLOGHANE CARHANE

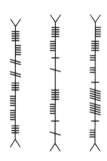

EQQEGGNI

MAQI MAQI

CARRATTIN

was she a friend
women fight
here among the ivy
now I begin to see   lust
                 in the ivy
women fighting
bees swarming

now we're all angry
should be

                 taking stock
                 minding cattle
was she a friend
thief of the grove of silence
lust
drains blood
boils my blood
was she a friend

CLOGHANE CARHANE
underneath his name

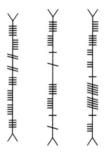

EQQEGGNI

MAQI MAQI

CARRATTIN

carpenter's work

it starts to make sense
hazel
it starts to make sense
alder
the most withered wood

the job in hand

clarity

cutting

the highest of bushes
ivy
nettles
the most decayed wood

it answers muster
the elm
the apple
forest & orchard
& the hazel

ABERNETHY

coltsfoot the apple that suckles
sun hoof the vine that strangles
sun horse the yew that sickens

ABERNETHY

quick   gentle

so hard to quell

elder

the hind   the hunt

quenched

elder

CHURCH OF THE 3 HOLY BRETHREN
LOCHGOILHEAD

H M U D A L I

little saint of whitethorn
little douser of wolf spark
welcome to the burial mounds

dear confessor of blood-red berries
sweet dweller of beehive cell
oaks make good gallow-trees

my heart
meagre

CHURCH OF THE 3 HOLY BRETHREN
LOCHGOILHEAD

H M U D A L I

bees have their own pollen auguries

there are thirteen

of blanching night

of swarming death

of chilling earth

of propagating plants

of lustrous herb

of the infirmity of tone

& six contained

in the thicket of letters

THE NORTHERN ISLES

BIRSAY

MONNORRANRR

her mouth music
mo norn

the breath she loves
voice wave

her horses & bands
the boast of peace

her great sorrow
what she leaves

a glow of anger
not her calling

BIRSAY

MAQITAM

a son
follows the breath of voice

sheltering
in bushes & rags

infirm
of energy

a third
of the great cycle

girning
to no response

BIRSAY

MAQI

a second son
twice blank

a ϕ
unheard

POOL

manifold the wheel
honey bees dancing
blush of the dying
breath of mares
wood brands burning
warriors at the breast
trees green leafing
world wheel whirling

BUCKQUOY SPINDLE WHORL

ENDDACTANIM

a circular charm for the breath
circular breath as charm

trembling groaning marvelling
to protect our heart
(beginning is unknown)
flame to marrow
breath path
of the voice

GURNESS BROCH

INEITTEMEN MATS

TEMENOS

last becomes first in ash womb

                            this place is for women

                  inside yew

                            a given thing to daughters

              aspen trembling

                            this place is for nieces

reddest fruit of her female she holly

              briar's holding

                            sanctuary for grandmothers

           wind silvered fir

                            set apart for the crone

         willow sap source

                            home to quine

                            all blood moon gathered

the unbreathing paid for with breathing things

SHETLAND TREE STORIES

CUNNINGSBURGH

DWDORN

oak alder elder rowan
the highest bush is only joiners' work
what is safe for cows hides butchers
the highest bush is only joiners' work
it's no use blustering
bright eyes look out for cattle

CUNNINGSBURGH

EHTECONMOR

aspen hawthorn holly hazel furze ash vine & elder
dear distinguished trembling friends
wolves slink behind bush & tree
three times we'll burn them
wolves tree & bush
cracking straight sweet limbs & nut & seed
become axle-tree
become stick
become poison
become axle & spoke
become blood

WHITENESS

we guard the heart
with floated wood & milk bowl

we cry grace
with legend of oaktree

we're kine calling
& otter selkies come

ACKNOWLEDGEMENTS

Many of these poems in earlier versions appeared in the following print & online journals & anthologies:

Arbolarium de los cinco continentes; Technicians of the Sacred: A range of poetries from Africa, America, Asia, Europe and Oceania; fourfold; Poems & Poetics; Jacket; Reliquiae; Nature and Language: Contemporary Poetry Series; and in two of my other collections *Tongues of Stone & Printed on Water.*

My grateful thanks to the editors.

My gratitude, as ever, to Morven Gregor for careful reading and for great patience.
Nine bows.

9 781999 971892